being born and growing older

VAN NOSTRAND REINHOLD LTD. TORONTO

NEW YORK, CINCINNATI, LONDON, MELBOURNE

being born and growing older

POEMS AND IMAGES ARRANGED BY BRUCE VANCE

LANGUAGE STUDY CENTRE, TORONTO

ISBN
paper 0 442 28910 3
cloth 0 442 28914 6

Library of Congress Catalogue Number: 73-152548

Printed and bound in Canada

Acknowledgments will be found on page 118.
An Index of Poems and Poets will be found on page 116.

design and photo research by Mary Cserepy

contents

to be born into

if . . .

contents

Death stands above me, whispering low

The world is too much with us

that the beautiful
are the most vulnerable . . .?

**The World Is a
Beautiful Place**

Lawrence
Ferlinghetti

The world is a beautiful place
                              to be born into
if you don't mind happiness
                          not always being
                                          so very much fun
    if you don't mind a touch of hell
                                  now and then
        just when everything is fine
                                  because even in heaven
            they don't sing
                            all the time

The world is a beautiful place
                              to be born into
if you don't mind some people dying
                              all the time
          or maybe only starving
                              some of the time
          which isn't half so bad
                              if it isn't you

Oh the world is a beautiful place
                              to be born into
          if you don't much mind
                    a few dead minds
          in the higher places
                    or a bomb or two
          now and then
                    in your upturned faces
     or such other improprieties
                         as our Name Brand society
               is prey to
                    with its men of distinction
          and its men of extinction
                    and its priests
          and other patrolmen
                              and its various segregations
          and congressional investigations
                         and other constipations
          that our fool flesh
                    is heir to

Yes the world is the best place of all
                              for a lot of such things as
          making the fun scene
                              and making the love scene
     and making the sad scene
                    and singing low songs and having inspirations
          and walking around
                         looking at everything
                                   and smelling flowers
          and goosing statues
                         and even thinking
                                   and kissing people and
          making babies and wearing pants
                                   and waving hats and
               dancing
                         and going swimming in rivers
          on picnics
                    in the middle of the summer
     and just generally
                    'living it up'

Yes
     but then right in the middle of it
                              comes the smiling

                    mortician

The Beautiful

W. H. Davies

Three things there are more beautiful
Than any man could wish to see:
The first it is a full-rigged ship
Sailing with all her sails set free;
The second, when the wind and sun
Are playing in a field of corn;
The third, a woman, young and fair,
Showing her child before it is born.

D-day Minus
Edwin Brock

Son, you have two more months
to live. On the sixteenth of December
1963, if the hospital has guessed
right, you will begin to die. By
the time you are old enough
to read this, you will be dead:
this is a process called communication.

You will not see the world at first:
you will touch flesh and you will cry.
Years later you will cry because
you see too much and touch too little.

You will be hungry for love, and love
will feed you; later, you will be
hungry for love. And love, in case
you do not understand, is the
condition you will come to fear.

Son, you are the third of my children;
the other two are dead, looking for
love. When you meet them, be
gentle; be gentle also with me;
and she who held you happily for
nine months: we too are looking for love.

And love, in case you do not understand,
is the grandeur that will kill you.
Have children soon, my son: everyone
should live for those nine months.
Afterwards, die in good company;
for dying is a lonely occupation.

**To the Anxious
Mother**
Valente
Malangatana

Into your arms I came
when you bore me, very anxious
you, who were so alarmed
at that monstrous moment
fearing that God might take me.
Everyone watched in silence
to see if the birth was going well
everyone washed their hands
to be able to receive the one who came from Heaven
and all the women were still and afraid.
But when I emerged
from the place where you sheltered me so long
at once I drew my first breath
at once you cried out with joy
the first kiss was my grandmother's.
And she took me at once to the place
where they kept me, hidden away
everyone was forbidden to enter my room
because everyone smelt bad
and I all fresh, fresh
breathed gently, wrapped in my napkins.
But grandmother, who seemed like a madwoman,
always looking and looking again
because the flies came at me
and the mosquitoes harried me
God who also watched over me
was my granny's friend.

**At the Washing
of My Son**
Su Tung P'o

Everybody wants an intelligent son.
My intelligence only got me into difficulties.
I want only a brave and simple boy,
Who, without trouble or resistance,
Will rise to the highest offices.

Copy
Richard Armour

His mother's eyes,
His father's chin,
His auntie's nose,
His uncle's grin,

His great-aunt's hair,
His grandma's ears,
His grandpa's mouth,
So it appears. . . .

Poor little tot,
Well may he moan.
He hasn't much
To call his own.

Death of a Son

*(who died in a
mental hospital
aged one)*

Jon Silkin

Something has ceased to come along with me.
Something like a person: something very like one.
And there was no nobility in it
Or anything like that.

Something was there like a one year
Old house, dumb as stone. While the near buildings
Sang like birds and laughed
Understanding the pact

They were to have with silence. But he
Neither sang nor laughed. He did not bless silence
Like bread, with words.
He did not forsake silence.

But rather, like a house in mourning
Kept the eye turned in to watch the silence while
The other houses like birds
Sang around him.

And the breathing silence neither
Moved nor was still.

I have seen stones: I have seen brick
But this house was made up of neither bricks nor stone
But a house of flesh and blood
With flesh of stone

And bricks for blood. A house
Of stones and blood in breathing silence with the other
Birds singing crazy on its chimneys.
But this was silence,

This was something else, this was
Hearing and speaking though he was a house drawn
Into silence, this was
Something religious in his silence,

Something shining in his quiet,
This was different, this was altogether something else:
Though he never spoke, this
Was something to do with death.

8

And then slowly the eye stopped looking
Inward. The silence rose and became still.
The look turned to the outer place and stopped,
   With the birds still shrilling around him.
   And as if he could speak

He turned over on his side with his one year
Red as a wound
He turned over as if he could be sorry for this
And out of his eyes two great tears rolled, like stones, and
   he died.

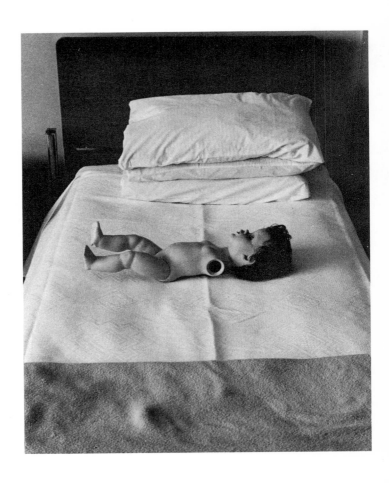

In Loving Remembrance
of
JOHN A. CAMERON
Died Nov. 27 1888.

The Children
William Carlos
Williams

Once in a while
we'd find a patch
of yellow violets

not many
but blue big blue
ones in

the cemetery woods
we'd pick
bunches of them

there was a family
named Foltette
a big family

with lots of children's graves
so we'd take

bunches of violets
and place one
on each headstone

Maternity
Alice Meynell

One wept whose only child was dead,
    Newborn, ten years ago.
'Weep not; he is in bliss,' they said.
    She answered, 'Even so.

'Ten years ago was born in pain
    A child, not now forlorn.
But oh, ten years ago, in vain,
    A mother, a mother was born.'

The Stunt Flier

John Updike

I come into my dim bedroom
innocently and my baby
is lying in her crib facedown;
just a hemisphere of the half-bald head
shows, and the bare feet, uncovered,
the small feet crossed at the ankles
like a dancer doing easily
a difficult step—or,
more exactly, like a cherub
planing through Heaven,
cruising at a middle altitude
through the cumulus of the tumbled covers,
which disclose the feet crossed
at the ankles à la small boys who,
exulting in their mastery of bicycles,
lift their hands from the handle bars
to demonstrate how easy gliding is.

**High Chair
and
Low Spirits**
Richard Armour

To feed the baby's quite a chore:
We plead and threaten, rant and roar.

We try to joke, we gently coo;
The joke's on us—the food is too.

To feed the baby's far from fun,
It's touch and goo until we're done.

Here comes a squall, his mouth is puckered. . . .
It's Baby's bib, but we are tuckered.

Goodbat Nightman

Roger McGough

God bless all policemen
and fighters of crime,
May thieves go to jail
for a very long time.

They've had a hard day
helping clean up the town,
Now they hang from the mantelpiece
both upside down.

A glass of warm blood
and then straight up the stairs,
Batman and Robin
are saying their prayers.

. . . .

They've locked all the doors
and they've put out the bat,
Put on their batjamas
(They like doing that)

They've filled their batwater-bottles
made their batbeds,
With two springy battresses
for sleepy batheads.

They're closing red eyes
and they're counting black sheep,
Batman and Robin
are falling asleep.

Fortune

Lawrence
Ferlinghetti

Fortune

has its cookies to give out

which is a good thing

since it's been a long time since

that summer in Brooklyn
when they closed off the street

one hot day
and the

FIREMEN

turned on their hoses

and all the kids ran out in it

in the middle of the street

and there were

maybe a couple dozen of us

out there

with the water squirting up
to the

sky

and all over
us

there was maybe only six of us
                                    kids altogether
                running around in our
                                    barefeet and birthday
                suits
                and I remember Molly but then

        the firemen stopped squirting their hoses
                all of a sudden and went
                                back in
                        their firehouse
                                and
                started playing pinochle again
                        just as if nothing
                                had ever
                                        happened

        while I remember Molly
                                looked at me and

        ran in

        because I guess really we were the only ones there

The Party

Reed
Whittemore

They served tea in the sandpile, together with
Mudpies baked on the sidewalk.
After tea
The youngest said that he had had a good dinner,
The oldest dressed for a dance,
And they sallied forth together with watering pots
To moisten a rusted fire truck on account of it
Might rain.

I watched from my study,
Thought of my part in these contributions to world
Gaiety, and resolved
That the very least acknowledgement I could make
Would be to join them;
     so we
All took our watering pots (filled with pies)
And poured tea on our dog. Then I kissed the children
And told them that when they grew up we would have
Real tea parties.
'That did be fun!' the youngest shouted, and ate pies
With wild surmise.

False Security

John Betjeman

I remember the dread with which I at a quarter past four
Let go with a bang behind me our house front door
And, clutching a present for my dear little hostess tight,
Sailed out for the children's party into the night
Or rather the gathering night. For still some boys
In the near municipal acres were making a noise
Shuffling in fallen leaves and shouting and whistling
And running past hedges of hawthorn, spikey and bristling.
And black in the oncoming darkness stood out the trees
And pink shone the ponds in the sunset ready to freeze
And all was still and ominous waiting for dark
And the keeper was ringing his closing bell in the park
And the arc lights started to fizzle and burst into mauve
As I climbed West Hill to the great big house in The Grove,
Where the children's party was and the dear little hostess.
But halfway up stood the empty house where the ghost is
I crossed to the other side and under the arc
Made a rush for the next kind lamp-post out of the dark
And so to the next and the next till I reached the top
Where the Grove branched off to the left. Then ready to drop
I ran to the ironwork gateway of number seven
Secure at last on the lamplit fringe of Heaven.
Oh who can say how subtle and safe one feels
Shod in one's children's sandals from Daniel Neal's,
Clad in one's party clothes made of stuff from Heal's?
And who can still one's thrill at the candle shine
On cakes and ices and jelly and blackcurrant wine,
And the warm little feel of my hostess's hand in mine?
Can I forget my delight at the conjuring show?
And wasn't I proud that I was the last to go?
Too overexcited and pleased with myself to know
That the words I heard my hostess's mother employ
To a guest departing, would ever diminish my joy,
I WONDER WHERE JULIA FOUND THAT STRANGE, RATHER COMMON LITTLE BOY?

School's Out
W. H. Davies

Girls scream,
   Boys shout;
Dogs bark,
   School's out.

Cats run,
   Horses shy;
Into trees
   Birds fly.

Babes wake
   Open-eyed;
If they can,
   Tramps hide.

Old man,
   Hobble home;
Merry mites,
   Welcome.

**For a
Junior School
Poetry Book**
Christopher
Middleton

The mothers are waiting in the yard.
Here come the children, fresh from school.
The mothers are wearing rumpled skirts.
What prim mouths, what wrinkly cheeks.
The children swirl through the air to them,
trailing satchels and a smell of chalk.

The children are waiting in the yard.
The mothers come stumbling out of school.
The children stare primly at them,
lace their shoes, pat their heads.
The mothers swirl through the air to cars.
The children crossly drive them home.

The mothers are coming.
The children are waiting.
The mothers had eyes that see
boiled eggs, wool, dung and bed.
The children have eyes that saw
owl and mountain and little mole.

Noisy Boys

Jack
Castiglione

Crash, bang!
What was that noise?
It's never the girls,
So it MUST be the boys!
They jump and run,
They have lots of fun.
Boys, boys, boys,
Noise, noise, noise!

My Parents Kept Me

Stephen Spender

My parents kept me from children who were rough
And who threw words like stones and who wore torn clothes.
Their thighs showed through rags. They ran in the street
And climbed cliffs and stripped by the country streams.

I feared more than tigers their muscles like iron
And their jerking hands and their knees tight on my arms.
I feared the salt coarse pointing of those boys
Who copied my lisp behind me on the road.

They were lithe, they sprang out behind hedges
Like dogs to bark at our world. They threw mud
And I looked another way, pretending to smile.
I longed to forgive them, yet they never smiled.

Whatfor
to 3 Who Stole
My Shovel
Phyllis Gotlieb

I wouldn't give a damn if some rum
soaked gaffer with whiskey breath and tobacco
whisker clutching his
dollar wage for cleaning my walk
in a chapped claw
bitten quick and rimmed black

had tucked it under his arm
homefree in an eyeblink
at the turn of my back
and sold three dollars worth for
fifty cents to price
the bottle, got him a gulp
to warm the long grey of unlife

but you with your young hands, clean clothes
crisp hair, clear eyes
straight backs, strong legs, whole skin

pups in the pink of cheek
needing nothing but honour
you make me sick.

**The Man Who
Finds That
His Son Has
Become a Thief**

Raymond Souster

Coming into the store at first angry
At the accusation, believing in
The word of his boy who has told him:
I didn't steal anything, honest.

Then becoming calmer, seeing that anger
Will not help in the business, listening painfully
As the other's evidence unfolds, so painfully slow.

Then seeing gradually that evidence
Almost as if tighten slowly around the neck
Of his son, at first vaguely circumstantial,
    then gathering damage,
Until there is present the unmistakable odour of guilt
Which seeps now into the mind and lays its poison.

Suddenly feeling sick and alone and afraid,
As if an unseen hand had slapped him in the face
For no reason whatsoever: wanting to get out
Into the street, the night, the darkness, anywhere to hide
The pain that must show in the face to these strangers,
    the fear.

It must be like this.
It could hardly be otherwise.

Original Sin on the Sussex Coast

John Betjeman

Now on this out of season afternoon
Day schools which cater for the sort of boy
Whose parents go by Pullman once a month
To do a show in town, pour out their young
Into the sharply red October light.
Here where The Drive and Buckhurst Road converge
I watch the rival gangs and am myself
A schoolboy once again in shivering shorts.
I see the dust of sherbet on the chin
Of Andrew Knox well-dress'd, well-born, well-fed,
Even at nine a perfect gentleman,
Willie Buchanan waiting at his side—
Another Scot, eruptions on his skin.
I hear Jack Drayton whistling from the fence
Which hides the copper domes of "Cooch Behar",
That was the signal. So there's no escape.
A race for Willow Way and jump the hedge
Behind the Granville Bowling Club? Too late.
They'll catch me coming out in Seapink Lane.
Across the Garden of Remembrance? No,
That would be blasphemy and bring bad luck.
Well then, I'm *for* it. Andrew's at me first,
He pinions me in that especial grip
His brother learned in Kobë from a Jap
(No chance for me against the Japanese).
Willie arrives and winds me with a punch
Plum in the tummy, grips the other arm.
"You're to be booted. Hold him steady, chaps!"
A wait for taking aim. Oh trees and sky!
Then crack against the column of my spine,
Blackness and breathlessness and sick with pain
I stumble on the asphalt. Off they go
Away, away, thank God, and out of sight
So that I lie quite still and climb to sense
Too out of breath and strength to make a sound.

Now over Polegate vastly sets the sun;
Dark rise the Downs from darker looking elms,
And out of Southern railway trains to tea
Run happy boys down various Station Roads,
Satchels of homework jogging on their backs,
So trivial and so healthy in the shade
Of these enormous Downs. And when they're home,
When the Post-Toasties mixed with Golden Shred
Does Mum, the Persil-user, still believe
That there's no Devil and that youth is bliss?
As certain as the sun behind the Downs
And quite as plain to see, the Devil walks.

**In Woods Where
Many Rivers Run**
Lawrence
Ferlinghetti

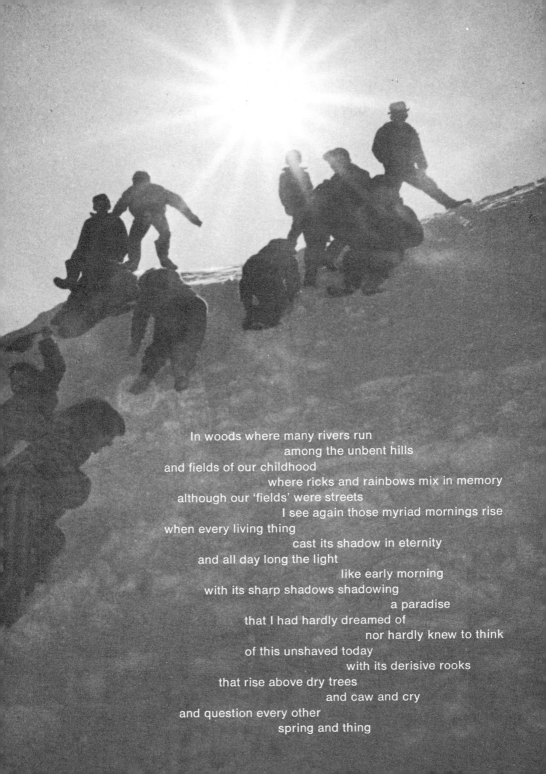

In woods where many rivers run
                          among the unbent hills
and fields of our childhood
                          where ricks and rainbows mix in memory
although our 'fields' were streets
                          I see again those myriad mornings rise
when every living thing
                          cast its shadow in eternity
and all day long the light
                          like early morning
with its sharp shadows shadowing
                          a paradise
that I had hardly dreamed of
                          nor hardly knew to think
of this unshaved today
                          with its derisive rooks
that rise above dry trees
                          and caw and cry
and question every other
                          spring and thing

Fern Hill

Dylan Thomas

Now as I was young and easy under the apple boughs
About the lilting house and happy as the grass was green,
   The night above the dingle starry,
     Time let me hail and climb
   Golden in the heydays of his eyes,
And honoured among wagons I was prince of the apple towns
And once below a time I lordly had the trees and leaves
     Trail with daisies and barley
   Down the rivers of the windfall light.

And as I was green and carefree, famous among the barns
About the happy yard and singing as the farm was home,
   In the sun that is young once only,
     Time let me play and be
   Golden in the mercy of his means,
And green and golden I was huntsman and herdsman,
       the calves
Sang to my horn, the foxes on the hills barked clear and cold,
     And the sabbath rang slowly
   In the pebbles of the holy streams.

All the sun long it was running, it was lovely, the hay-
Fields high as the house, the tunes from the chimneys,
     it was air
   And playing, lovely and watery
     And fire green as grass.
   And nightly under the simple stars
As I rode to sleep the owls were bearing the farm away,
All the moon long I heard, blessed among stables,
     the nightjars
   Flying with the ricks, and horses
     Flashing into the dark.

And then to awake, and the farm, like a wanderer white
With the dew, come back, the cock on his shoulder: it was all
   Shining, it was Adam and maiden,
     The sky gathered again
   And the sun grew round that very day.
So it must have been after the birth of the simple light
In the first, spinning place, the spellbound horses
     walking warm
   Out of the whinnying green stable
     On to the fields of praise.

And honoured among foxes and pheasants by the gay house
Under the new-made clouds and happy as the heart was long
   In the sun born over and over,
     I ran my heedless ways,
   My wishes raced through the house-high hay
And nothing I cared, at my sky blue trades, that time allows
In all his tuneful turning so few and such morning songs
   Before the children green and golden
     Follow him out of grace.

Nothing I cared, in the lamb white days, that time
     would take me
Up to the swallow-thronged loft by the shadow of my hand,
   In the moon that is always rising,
     Nor that riding to sleep
   I should hear him fly with the high fields
And wake to the farm forever fled from the childless land.
Oh as I was young and easy in the mercy of his means,
     Time held me green and dying
    Though I sang in my chains like the sea.

**Pastoral of the
City Streets**

A. M. Klein

I Between distorted forests, clapped into geometry,
in meadows of macadam,
heat-fluff-a-host-of-dandelions dances on the air.
Everywhere glares the sun's glare,
the asphalt shows hooves.

                In meadows of macadam
grazes the dray horse, nozzles his bag of pasture,
is peaceful. Now and then flicks through farmer straw
his ears, like pulpit-flowers; quivers
his hide; swishes his tempest tail
a black and sudden nightmare for the fly.
The sun shines, sun shines down
new harness on his withers, saddle, and rump.

On curbrock and on stairstump the clustered kids
resting let slide some afternoon: then restless
hop to the game of the sprung haunches; skid
to the safe place; jump up: stir a wind in the heats:
laugh, puffed and sweat-streaked.

O for the crystal stream!

Comes a friend's father
with his pet of a hose,
and plays the sidewalk black
cavelike and cool.

O crisscross beneath the spray, those pelting petals and peas
those white soft whisks
brushing off heat!
O underneath these acrobatic fountains
among the crystal,
like raindrops a sunshower of youngsters dance:
small-nippled self-hugged boys
and girls with water sheer, going *Ah* and *Ah*.

II   And at twilight,
the sun like a strayed neighbourhood creature
having been chased
back to its cover
the children count a last game, or talk, or rest,
beneath the bole of the tree of the single fruit of glass
now ripening,
a last game, talk, or rest,
until mothers, like evening birds call from the stoops.

**The Key of
the Kingdom**

Ed Reed

When we were children
We possessed the key to a kingdom
Such as this world has yet to see.
Wherever we went;
By lakes,
Pools
And streams,
In woods,
Meadows
And fields,
There was a world beyond belief
In which anything could be something else.
A world
Whose every corner
Would yield some new adventure or surprise.
A world
In which we ruled
And was ours alone.

Only we children had the key,
The key of the kingdom.

A world inhabited by goblins, ghosts and ghouls,
Dragons, trolls, witches, sorcerers,
Knights, fair damsels, wicked kings
And green-skinned, three-eyed floops.
A world of enchanted geography —
Magic Forests,
Glass mountains
And fountains of youth.

In this world
We held our castles
Made of T.V. boxes
Against marauding bands of Vikings
Armed with swords made of lattice
And shields taken from the tops of garbage cans.
We sailed with Columbus
Across the unchartered waters of a lily pond.
We descended.
With Captain Nemo
To 20,000 leagues beneath the bathwater.
We went west with the pioneers
By coaster wagon,
And to the East with Marco Polo
By tricycle.
We defied savage Indians
From the next block
And returned alive
In time for an afternoon nap.
We hunted fierce man-eating squirrels.
We dared damnation
By taking the trainer wheels
Off our first bicycle.
We did a zillion billion other brave.
Courageous.
Bold.
Fun things.

Now that we are older.
Wiser
And more mature
This kingdom no longer has our allegiance.
We have lost the key
And it has perished with the rust of misuse
And neglect.

Age is the grave yard
Of all our youthful hopes.
Dreams
And experiences.

The Playground
Michael Bedard

Up go the children, up the rungs
Of the swirly-slide
And down they come,
Then up again and winding round
They dash their laughter to the ground,
To the foot-pressed ground of trampled dust,
As up they go, so down they must.

In the shade of the slide of the swirlers wild
Are the string-strung horses, with each a child,
Creaking their riders to and fro,
As up the sliders down they go.

As if the creaking horses knew
As, coloured, swing they fro and to
And, patient, plunge by the swirling slide
As back the riders forth they ride.

The children pressing side on side
To swing the steeds or wind the slide,
Laughing and shrieking the sun away,
As children do, as children may,
Tramping the dust of the foot-pressed ground,
As up they go so must they down.

The swingers and sliders in passion bent
To slide and swing their youth are meant,
For up go the children, up the rungs
Of the swirly-slide . . . . . .

Then down they come.

As up they go so down they must
To the waiting ground and the swallowing dust.

Norfolk

John Betjeman

How did the Devil come? When first attack?
    These Norfolk lanes recall lost innocence,
The years fall off and find me walking back
    Dragging a stick along the wooden fence
Down this same path, where, forty years ago,
My father strolled behind me, calm and slow.

I used to fill my hand with sorrel seeds
    And shower him with them from the tops of stiles,
I used to butt my head into his tweeds
    To make him hurry down those languorous miles
Of ash and alder-shaded lanes, till here
Our moorings and the masthead would appear.

There after supper lit by lantern light
    Warm in the cabin I could lie secure
And hear against the polished sides at night
    The lap lap lapping of the weedy Bure,
A whispering and watery Norfolk sound
Telling of all the moonlit reeds around.

How did the Devil come? When first attack?
    The church is just the same, though now I know
Fowler of Louth restored it. Time, bring back
    The rapturous ignorance of long ago,
The peace, before the dreadful daylight starts,
Of unkept promises and broken hearts.

in Just-

e. e. cummings

in Just-
spring   when the world is mud-
luscious the little
lame balloonman

whistles   far   and wee
and eddieandbill come
running from marbles and
piracies and it's
spring

when the world is puddle-wonderful

the queer
old balloonman whistles
far   and   wee

and bettyandisbel come dancing

from hop-scotch and jump-rope and

it's
spring
and
      the
            goat-footed

balloonMan   whistles
far
and
wee

The
Horse Chestnut
Tree
Richard Eberhart

Boys in sporadic but tenacious droves
Come with sticks, as certainly as Autumn,
To assault the great horse chestnut tree.

There is a law governs their lawlessness.
Desire is in them for a shining amulet
And the best are those that are highest up.

They will not pick them easily from the ground.
With shrill arms they fling to the higher branches,
To hurry the work of nature for their pleasure.

I have seen them trooping down the street
Their pockets stuffed with chestnuts shucked, unshucked.
It is only evening keeps them from their wish.

Sometimes I run out in a kind of rage
To chase the boys away: I catch an arm,
Maybe, and laugh to think of being the lawgiver.

I was once such a young sprout myself
And fingered in my pocket the prize and trophy.
But still I moralize upon the day

And see that we, outlaws on God's property,
Fling out imagination beyond the skies,
Wishing a tangible good from the unknown.

And likewise death will drive us from the scene
With the great flowering world unbroken yet,
Which we held in idea, a little handful.

**Walnut-Leaf
Scent**

Laurence Binyon

In the high leaves of a walnut,
On the very topmost boughs,
A boy that climbed the branching bole
His cradled limbs would house.

On the airy bed that rocked him
Long, idle hours he'd lie
Alone with white clouds sailing
The warm blue of the sky.

I remember not what his dreams were;
But the scent of a leaf's enough
To house me higher than those high boughs
In a youth he knew not of,

In a light that no day brings now
But none can spoil or smutch,
A magic that I felt not then
And only now I touch.

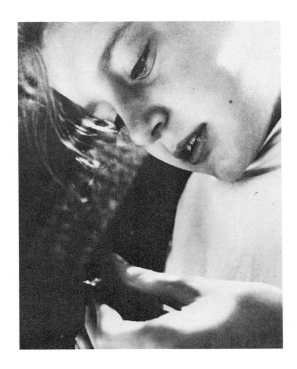

**The
Pennycandystore
beyond the El**

Lawrence
Ferlinghetti

The pennycandystore beyond the El
is where I first
         fell in love
               with unreality
Jellybeans glowed in the semi-gloom
of that september afternoon
A cat upon the counter moved among
               the licorice sticks
        and tootsie rolls
     and Oh Boy Gum

Outside the leaves were falling as they died

A wind had blown away the sun

A girl ran in
Her hair was rainy
Her breasts were breathless in the little room

Outside the leaves were falling
         and they cried
               Too soon! too soon!

l (a

e. e. cummings

l(a

le
af
fa

ll

s)
one
l

iness

To Margaret
Gerard Manley
Hopkins

Margarét, are you grieving
Over Goldengrove unleaving?
Leaves, like the things of man, you
With your fresh thoughts care for, can you?
Ah! as the heart grows older
It will come to such sights colder
By and by, nor spare a sigh
Though worlds of wanwood leafmeal lie;
And yet you will weep and know why.
Now no matter, child, the name:
Sorrow's springs are the same.
Nor mouth had, no nor mind, expressed
What heart heard of, ghost guessed:
It is the blight man was born for,
It is Margaret you mourn for.

Innocence
Irving Layton

How does one tell
one's fourteen-year-old daughter
that the beautiful
are the most vulnerable
and that a rage
tears at the souls
of humans
to corrupt innocence
and to smash butterflies
to see their wings
flutter in the sun
pulling weeds and flowers
from the soil:
and that all, all
go under the earth
to make room for more
weeds and flowers
— some more beautiful than others?

Tumbling-hair
e. e. cummings

Tumbling-hair
            picker of buttercups
                    violets

dandelions
And the big bullying daisies
                 through the field wonderful
with eyes a little sorry
Another comes
        also picking flowers

The Little Dancers
Laurence Binyon

Lonely, save for a few faint stars, the sky
Dreams; and lonely, below, the little street
Into its gloom retires, secluded and shy.
Scarcely the dumb roar enters this soft retreat;
And all is dark, save where come flooding rays
From a tavern window; there, to the brisk measure
Of an organ that down in an alley merrily plays,
Two children, all alone and no one by,
Holding their tattered frocks, thro' an airy maze
Of motion lightly threaded with nimble feet
Dance sedately; face to face they gaze,
Their eyes shining, grave with a perfect pleasure.

**To a Child Dancing
in the Wind**
W. B. Yeats

Dance there upon the shore;
What need have you to care
For wind or water's roar?
And tumble out your hair
That the salt drops have wet;
Being young you have not known
The fool's triumph, nor yet
Love lost as soon as won,
Nor the best labourer dead
And all the sheaves to bind.
What need have you to dread
The monstrous crying of wind?

**Seasonal
Phenomenon**

Richard Armour

The lifeguard is a man of brawn.
He has a streamlined swim suit on
That fits him like his very skin.
He is not fat, he is not thin;
It is, in fact, his lucky fate
To have no need to watch his weight.
His limbs are trim, his knees unknotted,
His tan is even and unspotted,
He has a profile like Adonis,
And as, with stately, godlike slowness
He regularly paces by,
He wins the soft, admiring eye,
Without half trying to, of each
And every female on the beach.

Oh, let him have his hour of glory —
This creature of a season — for he
Will, as the days grow short, grow sober.
Who cares for lifeguards in October?

**Ex-basketball
Player**

John Updike

Pearl Avenue runs past the high-school lot,
Bends with the trolley tracks, and stops, cut off
Before it has a chance to go two blocks,
At Colonel McComsky Plaza. Berth's Garage
Is on the corner facing west, and there,
Most days, you'll find Flick Webb, who helps Berth out.

Flick stands tall among the idiot pumps —
Five on a side, the old bubble-head style,
Their rubber elbows hanging loose and low.
One's nostrils are two S's, and his eyes
An E and O. And one is squat, without
A head at all — more of a football type.

Once Flick played for the high-school team, the Wizards.
He was good: in fact, the best. In '46
He bucketed three hundred ninety points,
A county record still. The ball loved Flick.
I saw him rack up thirty-eight or forty
In one home game. His hands were like wild birds.

He never learned a trade, he just sells gas,
Checks oil, and changes flats. Once in a while,
As a gag, he dribbles an inner tube,
But most of us remember anyway.
His hands are fine and nervous on the lug wrench.
It makes no difference to the lug wrench, though.

Off work, he hangs around Mae's Luncheonette.
Grease-grey and kind of coiled, he plays pinball,
Sips lemon cokes, and smokes those thin cigars;
Flick seldom speaks to Mae, just sits and nods
Beyond her face towards bright applauding tiers
Of Necco Wafers, Nibs, and Juju Beads.

Homework for Annabelle

Phyllis McGinley

$A = bh$ over 2.
   3.14 is π.
But I'd forgotten, if I ever knew,
   What R's divided by.
Though I knew once, I'd forgotten clean
What a girl must study to reach fifteen—
How V is Volume and M's for Mass,
And the hearts of the young are brittle as glass.

I had forgotten, and half with pride,
   Fifteen's no field of clover.
So here I sit at Annabelle's side,
   Learning my lessons over.
For help is something you have to give
When daughters are faced with the Ablative
Or first encounter in any school
Immutable gender's mortal rule.

Day after day for a weary spell,
   When the dusk has pitched its tents,
I sit with a book and Annabelle
   At the hour of confidence
And rummage for lore I had long consigned
To cobwebby attics of my mind,
Like: For the Radius, write down R,
The Volga's a river, Vega's a star,
Brazil's in the Tropic of Capricorn,
And heart is a burden that has to be borne.

Oh, high is the price of parenthood,
   And daughters may cost you double.
You dare not forget, as you thought you could,
   That youth is a plague and trouble.
N times 7 is $7n$—
Here I go learning it all again:
The climates of continents tend to vary,
The verb "to love" 's not auxiliary,
Tomorrow will come and today will pass,
But the hearts of the young are brittle as glass.

The Conventionalist

Stevie Smith

Fourteen-year-old, why must you giggle and dote,
Fourteen-year-old, why are you such a goat?
I'm fourteen years old, that is the reason,
I giggle and dote in season.

The Tea Shop

Ezra Pound

The girl in the tea shop
    Is not so beautiful as she was,
The August has worn against her.
She does not get up the stairs so eagerly;
Yes, she also will turn middle-aged,
And the glow of youth that she spread about us
    As she brought us our muffins
Will be spread about us no longer.
    She also will turn middle-aged.

old age

e. e. cummings

old age sticks
up Keep
Off
signs)&

youth yanks them
down(old
age
cries No

Tres)&(pas)
youth laughs
(sing
old age

scolds Forbid
den Stop
Must
n't Don't

&)youth goes
right on
gr
owing old

Icarus
Irving Layton

His friends drudged in an airplane factory.
The theory of speed was their sweaty talk;
And one who reclaimed rust machinery
Swore men hereafter would not run or walk.
Another crowed, pointing to his watch: "Feet?
As sure as I'm staring at Time's own face
Our offspring shall be a limbless race,
Hopping in crystal ships from street to street."
Icarus went on working on his wings.
Really be despised their tame discussion;
He'd fly, but as a god towards the sun;
And rubbing the strong wax into the strings,
He leaped into the air—to hear the chorus
Of dismayed cries: "You're bluffing, Icarus!"

**Landscape
with the
Fall of Icarus**
William Carlos
Williams

According to Brueghel
when Icarus fell
it was spring

a farmer was ploughing
his field
the whole pageantry

of the year was
awake tingling
near

the edge of the sea
concerned
with itself

sweating in the sun
that melted
the wings' wax

unsignificantly
off the coast
there was

a splash quite unnoticed
this was
Icarus drowning

The Average
W. H. Auden

His peasant parents killed themselves with toil
To let their darling leave a stingy soil
For any of those smart professions which
Encourage shallow breathing, and grow rich.

The pressure of their fond ambition made
Their shy and country-loving child afraid
No sensible career was good enough,
Only a hero could deserve such love.

So here he was without maps or supplies,
A hundred miles from any decent town;
The desert glared into his blood-shot eyes;

The silence roared displeasure: looking down,
He saw the shadow of an Average Man
Attempting the exceptional, and ran.

Warren Pryor
Alden Nowlan

When every pencil meant a sacrifice
his parents boarded him at school in town,
slaving to free him from the stony fields,
the meagre acreage that bore them down.

They blushed with pride when, at his graduation,
they watched him picking up the slender scroll,
his passport from the years of brutal toil
and lonely patience in a barren hole.

When he went in the Bank their cups ran over.
They marvelled how he wore a milk-white shirt
work days and jeans on Sundays. He was saved
from their thistle-strewn farm and its red dirt.

And he said nothing. Hard and serious
like a young bear inside his teller's cage,
his axe-hewn hands upon the paper bills
aching with empty strength and throttled rage.

Sketch 48 b. 11

Ezra Pound

At the age of 27
Its home mail is still opened by its maternal parent
And its office mail may be opened by
      its parent of the opposite gender.
It is an officer,
      and a gentleman,
          and an architect.

Who's Who

W. H. Auden

A shilling life will give you all the facts:
How Father beat him, how he ran away,
What were the struggles of his youth, what acts
Made him the greatest figure of his day:
Oh how he fought, fished, hunted, worked all night,
Though giddy, climbed new mountains; named a sea:
Some of the last researchers even write
Love made him weep pints like you and me.

With all his honours on, he sighed for one
Who, say astonished critics, lived at home;
Did little jobs about the house with skill
And nothing else; could whistle; would sit still
Or potter round the garden; answered some
Of his long marvellous letters but kept none.

**In Goya's
Greatest
Scenes**

Lawrence
Ferlinghetti

In Goya's greatest scenes we seem to see
                                                    the people of the world
                exactly at the moment when
                    they first attained the title of
                                                    'suffering humanity'
                They writhe upon the page
                                                    in a veritable rage
                                                        of adversity
            Heaped up
                groaning with babies and bayonets
                                                    under cement skies
                in an abstract landscape of blasted trees
                bent statues bats wings and beaks
                        slippery gibbets
                cadavers and carnivorous cocks
                and all the final hollering monsters
                    of the
                        'imagination of disaster'
                they are so bloody real
                                    it is as if they really still existed

And they do

        Only the landscape is changed

They still are ranged along the roads
      plagued by legionaires
              false windmills and demented roosters

They are the same people
                only further from home
    on freeways fifty lanes wide
        on a concrete continent
             spaced with bland billboards
          illustrating imbecile illusions of happiness

The scene shows fewer tumbrils
        but more maimed citizens
                in painted cars
     and they have strange license plates
   and engines
       that devour America

T

TRIBUTES TO

HENRY FORD

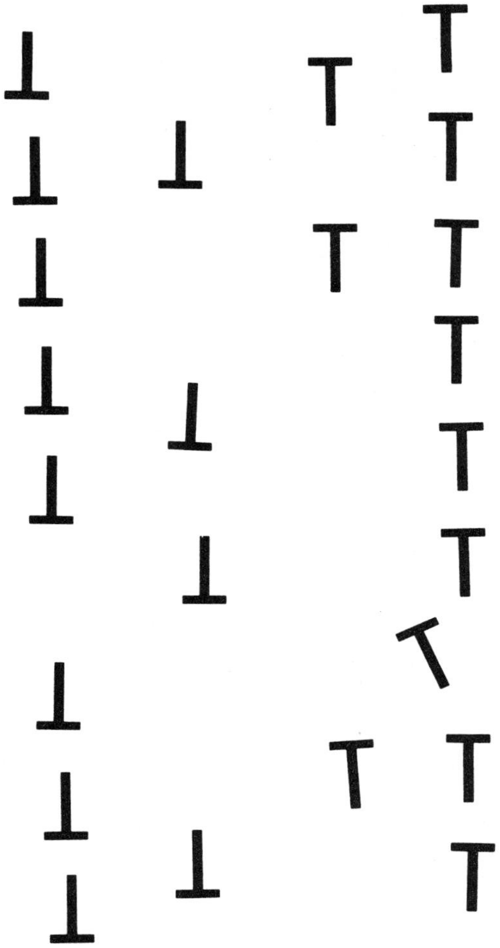

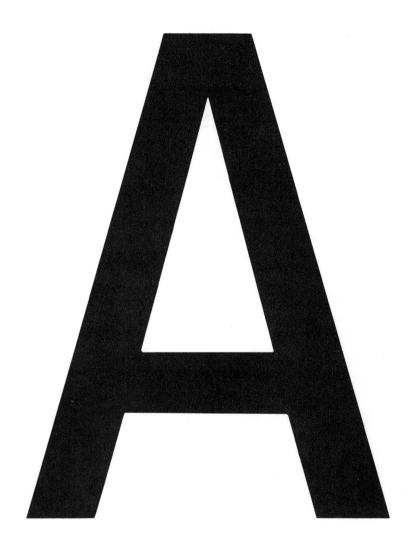

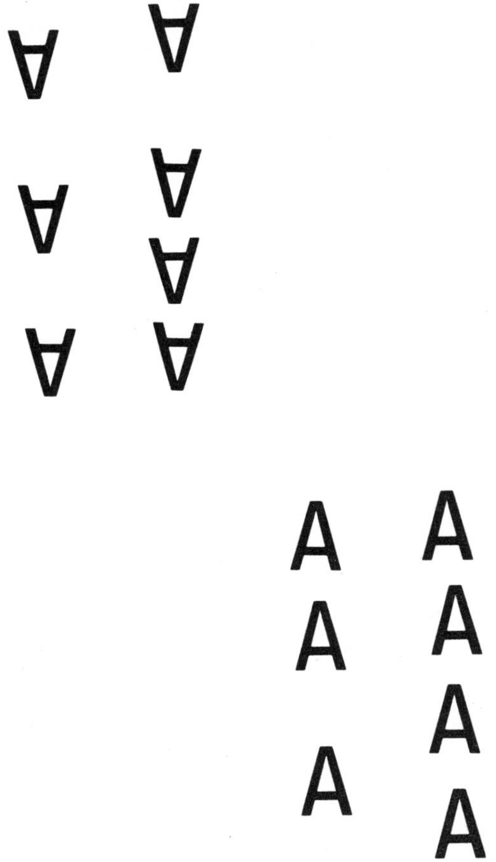

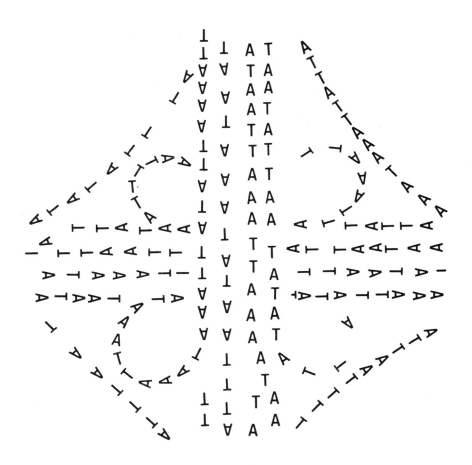

Richard Kostelanetz

**Southbound on
the Freeway**
May Swenson

A tourist came in from Orbitville,
parked in the air, and said:

The creatures of this star
are made of metal and glass.

Through the transparent parts
you can see their guts.

Their feet are round and roll
on diagrams—or long

measuring tapes—dark
with white lines.

They have four eyes.
The two in the back are red.

Sometimes you can see a 5-eyed
one, with a red eye turning

on the top of his head.
He must be special—

the others respect him,
and go slow,

when he passes, winding
among them from behind.

They all hiss as they glide,
like inches, down the marked

tapes. Those soft shapes,
shadowy inside

the hard bodies—are they
their guts or their brains?

**Meditation on
the A30**

John Betjeman

A man on his own in a car
    Is revenging himself on his wife;
He opens the throttle and bubbles with dottle
    And puffs at his pitiful life.

"She's losing her looks very fast,
    She loses her temper all day;
That lorry won't let me get past,
    This Mini is blocking my way.

"Why can't you step on it and shift her!
    I can't go on crawling like this!
At breakfast she said she wished I was dead—
    Thank heavens we don't have to kiss.

"I'd like a nice blonde on my knee
    And one who won't argue or nag.
Who dares to come hooting *at me*?
    I only give way to a Jag.

"You're barmy or plastered, I'll pass you, you bastard—
    I *will* overtake you. I *will*!"
As he clenches his pipe, his moment is ripe
    And the corner's accepting its kill.

Superman

John Updike

I drive my car to supermarket,
   The way I take is superhigh,
A superlot is where I park it,
   And Super Suds are what I buy.

Supersalesmen sell me tonic—
   Super-Tone-O, for Relief.
The planes I ride are supersonic.
   In trains, I like the Super Chief.

Supercilious men and women
   Call me superficial—*me*,
Who so superbly learned to swim in
   Supercolossality.

Superphosphate-fed foods feed me;
   Superservice keeps me new.
Who would dare to supersede me,
   Super-super-superwho?

Daniel at
Breakfast
Phyllis
McGinley

His paper propped against the electric toaster
   (Nicely adjusted to his morning use),
Daniel at breakfast studies world disaster
   And sips his orange juice.

The words dismay him. Headlines shrilly chatter
   Of famine, storm, death, pestilence, decay.
Daniel is gloomy, reaching for the butter.
   He shudders at the way

War stalks the planet still, and men know hunger,
   Go shelterless, betrayed, may perish soon.
The coffee's weak again. In sudden anger
   Daniel throws down his spoon

And broods a moment on the kitchen faucet
   The plumber mended, but has mended ill;
Recalls tomorrow means a dental visit,
   Laments the grocery bill.

Then, having shifted from his human shoulder
   The universal woe, he drains his cup,
Rebukes the weather (surely turning colder),
   Crumples his napkin up
And, kissing his wife abruptly at the door,
Stamps fiercely off to catch the 8:04.

Women Who Are Hard Inside

Phyllis Gotlieb

Women who are hard inside and soft outside
roar out in cars that are soft inside and hard outside
into the soft outside ten o'clock morning air
from between houses like toyboxes emptied of their
excuses for existence, ride over the stunning
asphalt under incandescent April in slugwhite
carcoats and leatherpalmed driving gloves, hair
bright as peroxide to catch
opaline light,
and
    down
        down
            down to the dressmaker to match
buttons with great exactitude and cunning.

Pendulum

John Updike

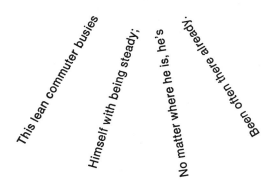

This lean commuter busies

Himself with being steady;

No matter where he is, he's

Been often there already.

**In a Station
of the Metro**
Ezra Pound

The apparition of these faces in the crowd;
Petals on a wet, black bough.

Things Made by Iron

D. H. Lawrence

Things made by iron and handled by steel
are born dead, they are shrouds, they soak life out of us.
Till after a long time, when they are old
    and have steeped in our life
they begin to be soothed and soothing:
    then we throw them away.

New Houses,
New Clothes —
D. H. Lawrence

New houses, new furniture, new streets,
    new clothes, new sheets
everything new and machine-made sucks life out of us
and makes us cold, makes us lifeless
the more we have.

Try Brillo on
the Slimy Stove
Phyllis Gotlieb

In toaster and rotisserie
an image in various disguises
boils on the morning air
in the twin chrome globes of the coffee pot
read the augury:

study the rust stains in the sink
from the twisted bowels divine
of the disembowelled washingmachine
what mark or magic it will take
of turn-three-times and point with Pride-
soaked rag to the shiny dinette in easy
instalments to make
resolving the greasy queasy
congruence of discrete imagery
into the image of integrity.

Cross my palm with Silvo: I see
a bright stranger tear
her plated hair—

O Lord! It's me!

Commercial Bank
A. M. Klein

Flowering jungle, where all fauna meet
crossing the marbled pool to thickets whence
the prompted parrots, alien-voiced, entreat
the kernel'd hoard, the efflorescent pence,—

wondrous your caves, whose big doors must be rolled
for entrance, and whose flora none can seek
against the armed unicorn, furred blue and gold,
against the vines fatal, or the berries that touched, shriek.

How quiet is your shade with broad green leaves!
Yet is it jungle-quiet which deceives:
toothless, with drawn nails, the beasts paw your ground—
O, the fierce deaths expiring with no sound!

**The World Is Too
Much with Us**
William Wordsworth

The world is too much with us; late and soon,
Getting and spending, we lay waste our powers:
Little we see in Nature that is ours;
We have given our hearts away, a sordid boon!
This Sea that bares her bosom to the moon;
The winds that will be howling at all hours,
And are up-gathered now like sleeping flowers;
For this, for everything, we are out of tune;
It moves us not.—Great God! I'd rather be
A Pagan suckled in a creed outworn;
So might I, standing on this pleasant lea,
Have glimpses that would make me less forlorn;
Have sight of Proteus rising from the sea;
Or hear old Triton blow his wreathèd horn.

Richard Cory
Edwin Arlington
Robinson

Whenever Richard Cory went down town,
We people on the pavement looked at him:
He was a gentleman from sole to crown,
Clean favoured, and imperially slim.

And he was always quietly arrayed,
And he was always human when he talked;
But still he fluttered pulses when he said,
"Good-morning," and he glittered when he walked.

And he was rich—yes, richer than a king—
And admirably schooled in every grace:
In fine, we thought that he was everything
To make us wish that we were in his place.

So on we worked, and waited for the light,
And went without the meat, and cursed the bread;
And Richard Cory, one calm summer night,
Went home and put a bullet through his head.

Oh Friend!
William Wordsworth

O friend! I know not which way I must look
For comfort, being, as I am, opprest,
To think that now our life is only drest
For show; mean handy-work of craftsman, cook,
Or groom!—We must run glittering like a brook
In the open sunshine, or we are unblest:
The wealthiest man among us is the best:
No grandeur now in nature or in book
Delights us. Rapine, avarice, expense,
This is idolatry; and these we adore:
Plain living and high thinking are no more:
The homely beauty of the good old cause
Is gone; our peace, our fearful innocence,
And pure religion breathing household laws.

**Public-House
Confidence**

Norman Cameron

Well, since you're from the other side of town,
I'll tell you how I hold a soft job down,
In the designing-rooms and laboratory
I'm dressed in overalls, and so pretend
To be on business from the factory.
The workmen think I'm from the other end.
The in-betweens and smart commission-men
Believe I must have some pull with the boss.
So, playing off the spanner against the pen
I never let the rumour get across
Of how I am no use at all to either
And draw the pay of both for doing neither.

The Ordinary Man

Robert Service

If you and I should chance to meet,
I guess you wouldn't care;
I'm sure you'd pass me in the street
As if I wasn't there;
You'd never look me in the face,
My modest mug to scan,
Because I'm just a commonplace
    And Ordinary Man.

But then, it may be, you are too
A guy of every day,
Who does the job he's told to do
And takes the wife his pay;
Who makes a home and kids his care,
And works with pick or pen. . . .
Why, Pal, I guess we're just a pair
    Of Ordinary Men.

We plug away and make no fuss,
Our feats are never crowned;
And yet it's common coves like us
Who make the world go round.
And as we steer a steady course
By God's predestined plan,
Hats off to that almighty Force:
    THE ORDINARY MAN.

The Suit
Leonard Cohen

I am locked in a very expensive suit
old elegant and enduring
Only my hair has been able to get free
but someone has been leaving
their dandruff in it
Now I will tell you
all there is to know about optimism
Each day in hub cap mirror
in soup reflection
in other people's spectacles
I check my hair
for an army of alpinists
for Indian rope trick masters
for tangled aviators
for dove and albatross
for insect suicides
for abominable snowmen
I check my hair
for aerialists of every kind
Dedicated as an automatic elevator
I comb my hair for possibilities
I stick my neck out
I lean illegally from locomotive windows
and only for the barber
do I wear a hat

On My
Thirty-third
Birthday
Lord Byron

Through life's dull road, so dim and dirty,
I have dragg'd to three-and-thirty.
What have these years left to me?
Nothing—except thirty-three.

First Fig

Edna St. Vincent
Millay

My candle burns at both ends;
   It will not last the night;
But ah, my foes, and oh, my friends—
   It gives a lovely light!

In Golden Gate
Park That Day

Lawrence
Ferlinghetti

In Golden Gate Park that day
      a man and his wife were coming along
  thru the enormous meadow
      which was the meadow of the world
He was wearing green suspenders
    and carrying an old beat-up flute
        in one hand
  while his wife had a bunch of grapes
      which she kept handing out
        individually
     to various squirrels
        as if each
      were a little joke

And then the two of them came on
     thru the enormous meadow
which was the meadow of the world
      and then
   at a very still spot where the trees dreamed
   and seemed to have been waiting thru all time
        for them
    they sat down together on the grass
      without looking at each other
   and ate oranges
     without looking at each other
       and put the peels
   in a basket which they seemed
      to have brought for that purpose
   without looking at each other

And then
              he took his shirt and undershirt off
        but kept his hat on
                  sideways
                      and without saying anything
          fell asleep under it
                    And his wife just sat there looking
at the birds which flew about
        calling to each other
                in the stilly air
        as if they were questioning existence
                  or trying to recall something forgotten

But then finally
           she too lay down flat
                and just lay there looking up
                      at nothing
        yet fingering the old flute
                which nobody played
        and finally looking over
                at him
      without any particular expression
                except a certain awful look
        of terrible depression

Is It Far to Go?
C. Day Lewis

Is it far to go?
 A step — no further.

Is it hard to go?
 Ask the melting snow,
 The eddying feather.

What can I take there?
 Not a hank, not a hair.

What shall I leave behind?
 Ask the hastening wind,
 The fainting star.

Shall I be gone long?
 For ever and a day.

To whom there belong?
 Ask the stone to say,
 Ask my song.

Who will say farewell?
 The beating bell.

Will anyone miss me?
 That I dare not tell —
 Quick, Rose, and kiss me.

Where Lies the Land

Arthur Hugh Clough

Where lies the land to which the ship would go?
Far, far ahead, is all her seamen know.
And where the land she travels from? Away,
Far, far behind, is all that they can say.

On sunny noons upon the deck's smooth face,
Linked arm in arm, how pleasant here to pace;
Or, o'er the stern reclining, watch below
The foaming wake far widening as we go.

On stormy nights when wild north-westers rave,
How proud a thing to fight with wind and wave!
The dripping sailor on the reeling mast
Exults to bear, and scorns to wish it past.

Where lies the land to which the ship would go?
Far, far ahead, is all her seamen know.
And where the land she travels from? Away,
Far, far behind, is all that they can say.

I Have Always Known
Narihira

I have always known
That at last I would
Take this road, but yesterday
I did not know that it would be today.

Song
Alfred,
Lord Tennyson

Who can say
Why Today
Tomorrow will be yesterday?
Who can tell
Why to smell
The violet, recalls the dewy prime
Of youth and buried time?
The cause is nowhere found in rhyme.

Into My Heart
A. E. Housman

Into my heart an air that kills
    From yon far country blows:
What are those blue remembered hills,
    What spires, what farms are those?

That is the land of lost content,
    I see it shining plain:
The happy highways where I went
    And cannot come again.

Sic Vita

Henry King

Like to the falling of a star,
Or as the flights of eagles are,
Or like the fresh spring's gaudy hue,
Or silver drops of morning dew,
Or like a wind that chafes the flood,
Or bubbles which on water stood:
Even such is man, whose borrowed light
Is straight called in, and paid to night.
    The wind blows out, the bubble dies;
    The spring entombed in autumn lies;
    The dew dries up, the star is shot;
    The flight is past, and man forgot.

103

**Letter to a
Conceivable
Great-Grandson**

Earle Birney

Perhaps it makes more
                    sense
                        in your eye
All I can tell you is
                how it looks from
                            here
For a while
            we made our brightest kids into
postmen   they dropped aircards
                            daily
marked *Urgent—*   DEATH!
until some dawn they'd flip
                        a card
and find their own ad-
dress
Now we've got automation   Our
                            letters
are set to de
            liver them
                    selves
                            fast
                            er than
meteors   Soon we'll be
sending wholemanuscriptsprepaidtothe
planets
But what's crazy for real is
we're so damned busy no
body has time to de   what
                    cipher
language it is we're   iting
                    r
                    w
All I can hope is

you'll be able to   make   it   out
with what   you   use
            ever
for an eye

**A Mad Poem
Addressed to
My Nephews
and Nieces**

Po Chü-i

The World cheats those who cannot read;
I, happily, have mastered script and pen.
The World cheats those who hold no office;
I am blessed with high official rank.
Often the old have much sickness and pain;
With me, luckily, there is not much wrong.
People when they are old are often burdened with ties;
But *I* have finished with marriage and giving in marriage.
No changes happen to jar the quiet of my mind;
No business comes to impair the vigour of my limbs.
Hence it is that now for ten years
Body and soul have rested in hermit peace.
And all the more, in the last lingering years
What I shall need are very few things.
A single rug to warm me through the winter;
One meal to last me the whole day.
It does not matter that my house is rather small;
One cannot sleep in more than one room!
It does not matter that I have not many horses;
One cannot ride on two horses at once!
As fortunate as me among the people of the world
Possibly one would find seven out of ten.
As contented as me among a hundred men
Look as you may, you will not find one.
In the affairs of others even fools are wise;
In their own business even sages err.
To no one else would I dare to speak my heart.
So my wild words are addressed to my nephews and nieces.

The Reckoning
Robert Service

It's fine to have a blow-out in a fancy restaurant,
With terrapin and canvas-back and all the wine you want;
To enjoy the flowers and music, watch the pretty women pass,
Smoke a choice cigar, and sip the wealthy water in your glass.
It's bully in a high-toned joint to eat and drink your fill,
But it's quite another matter when you
                                        Pay the bill.

It's great to go out every night on fun or pleasure bent;
To wear your glad rags always and to never save a cent;
To drift along regardless, have a good time every trip;
To hit the high spots sometimes, and to let your chances slip;
To know you're acting foolish, yet to go on fooling still,
Till Nature calls a show-down, and you
                                        Pay the bill.

Time has got a little bill — get wise while yet you may,
For the debit side's increasing in a most alarming way;
The things you had no right to do, the things
        you should have done,
They're all put down; it's up to you to pay for every one.
So eat, drink and be merry, have a good time if you will,
But God help you when the time comes, and you
                                        Foot the bill.

**Who Killed
Lawless Lean?**
Stevie Smith

The parrot
Is eating a carrot
In his cage in the garret

Why is the parrot's
Cage in the garret?
He is not a sage
Parrot: his words enrage.

Downstairs
In his bed
Lies the head
Of the family
He is dead.

And the brothers gather
Mutter utter would rather
Forget
The words the parrot
Said.

When high in his cage swinging
From the lofty ceiling
Sat the pet screaming:
'Who killed Lawless Lean?'
It was not at all fitting.

So they put the parrot
In his cage in the garret
And gave him a carrot
To keep him quiet.
He should be glad they did not wring his neck.

Death Snips
Proud Men

Carl Sandburg

Death is stronger than all the governments because the governments are men and men die and then death laughs: Now you see 'em, now you don't.

Death is stronger than all proud men and so death snips proud men on the nose, throws a pair of dice and says: Read 'em and weep.

Death sends a radiogram every day: When I want you I'll drop in — and then one day he comes with a master-key and lets himself in and says: We'll go now.

Death is a nurse mother with big arms: 'Twon't hurt you at all; it's your time now; you just need a long sleep, child; what have you had anyhow better than sleep?

On Death

Walter Savage Landor

Death stands above me, whispering low
    I know not what into my ear;
Of his strange language all I know
    Is, there is not a word of fear.

A Leaf Treader
Robert Frost

I have been treading on leaves all day until I am autumn-
   tired.
God knows all the colour and form of leaves I have trodden
   on and mired.
Perhaps I have put forth too much strength and been too
   fierce from fear.
I have safely trodden underfoot the leaves of another year.

All summer long they were over head, more lifted up than I.
To come to their final place in earth they had to pass me by.
All summer long I thought I heard them threatening under
   their breath.
And when they came it seemed with a will to carry me with
   them to death.

They spoke to the fugitive in my heart as if it were leaf
   to leaf.
They tapped at my eyelids and touched my lips with an
   invitation to grief.
But it was no reason I had to go because they had to go.
Now up my knee to keep on top of another year of snow.

Because I
Could Not
Stop for Death

Emily Dickinson

Because I could not stop for Death,
He kindly stopped for me;
The carriage held but just ourselves
And Immortality.

We slowly drove, he knew no haste,
And I had put away
My labour, and my leisure too,
For his civility.

We passed the school where children played
At wrestling in a ring;
We passed the fields of gazing grain,
We passed the setting sun.

We paused before a house that seemed
A swelling of the ground;
The roof was scarcely visible,
The cornice but a mound.

Since then 't is centuries; but each
Feels shorter than the day
I first surmised the horses' heads
Were toward eternity.

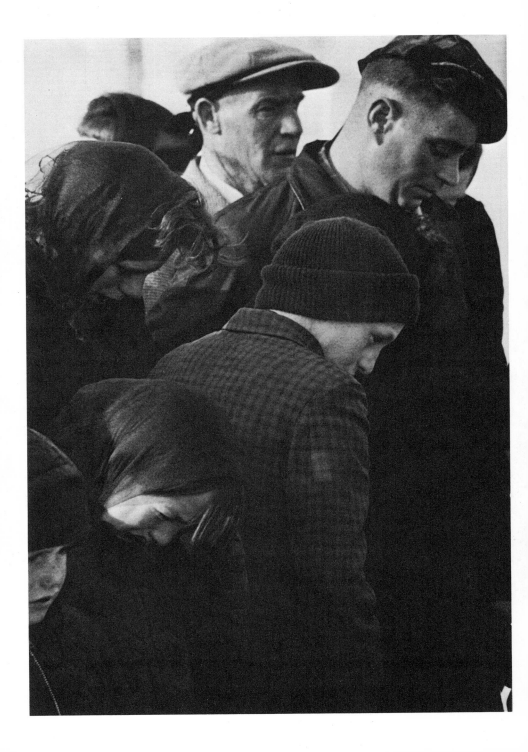

Come Not, When I Am Dead

Alfred,
Lord Tennyson

Come not, when I am dead,
    To drop thy foolish tears upon my grave,
To trample round my fallen head,
    And vex the unhappy dust thou wouldst not save.
There let the wind sweep and the plover cry;
      But thou, go by.

Child, if it were thine error or thy crime
    I care no longer, being all unblest:
Wed whom thou wilt, but I am sick of Time,
    And I desire to rest.
Pass on, weak heart, and leave me where I lie:
      Go by, go by.

Epitaph
Lascelles
Abercrombie

Sir, you should notice me: I am the Man:
I am Good Fortune: I am satisfied.
All I desired, more than I could desire,
I have: everything has gone right with me.
Life was a hiding-place that played me false;
I croucht ashamed, and still was seen and scorned:
But now I am not seen. I was a fool,
And now I know what wisdom dare not know:
For I know Nothing. I was a slave, and now
I have ungoverned freedom, and the wealth
That cannot be conceived: for I have Nothing.
I lookt for beauty and I longed for rest,
And now I have perfection: nay, I am
Perfection: I am Nothing, I am dead.

if
Haroldo
de Campos

if
to be born
to die   to be born
to die   to be born   to die
                  to be born   to die again   to be reborn
                                to die again   to be reborn
                                                to die again
                                                        again

                                again
                        not to be born
            not to be dead   not to be born
not to be dead   not to be born   not to be dead
                                to be born to die to be born
                                to die to be born
                                to die
                                if

115

index of poems and poets

acknowledgments

Grateful acknowledgement is made to the following for permission to use the copyrighted material indicated below. Every reasonable care has been taken to correctly acknowledge copyright ownership. The author and publisher would welcome information that will enable them to rectify any errors or omissions in succeeding printings.

the poetry

George Allen & Unwin Ltd.: For "A Mad Poem Addressed to My Nephews and Nieces" by Arthur Waley, from *Chinese Poems*.

Earnest Benn Ltd.: For "The Ordinary Man" by Robert Service from *Songs of a Sun Lover*.

Edwin Brock.: For "D-day Minus".

Jonathan Cape Ltd.: For "Is it Far to Go?" by C. Day Lewis, from *Collected Poems 1954*, © by the Hogarth Press. For "The Beautiful", and "School's Out" by W. H. Davies, from *The Complete Poems of W. H. Davies,* © by Mrs. H. M. Davies.

Centaur Press Ltd.: For "Death" by W. S. Landor from *Death* edited by Geoffrey Grigson.

Chatto and Windus Ltd.: For "Death of a Son" by John Silkin, from *Poems New and Selected.* For "Horse Chestnut Tree" by Richard Eberhart.

J. M. Dent & Sons Ltd.: For "Fern Hill" by Dylan Thomas from *Collected Poems of Dylan Thomas,* © Trustees for the copyrights of the late Dylan Thomas.

Norma Millay Ellis: For "First Fig" by Edna St. Vincent Millay from *Collected Poems,* published by Harper & Row, copyright 1922, 1950.

Faber & Faber Limited: For "My Parents Kept Me" by Stephen Spender from *Collected Poems.* For "The Average" and "Who's Who" by W. H. Auden from *Collected Shorter Poems 1927-1957.*

Harper & Row, Publishers, Inc.: For "Ex-Basketball Player" by John Updike from *The Carpentered Hen and Other Tame Creatures,* copyright 1957 (originally appeared in *The New Yorker*). For "Superman" by John Updike, copyright 1955. For "Pendulum" by John Updike, copyright 1958.

Harcourt Brace Jovanovich Inc.: For "in Just", copyright 1923, 1951, by e. e. cummings, reprinted from *Poems 1923-1954.* For "l(a" from *95 Poems* © 1958 by e. e. cummings. For "old age" © 1950 by e. e. cummings, reprinted from, *95 Poems;* "Tumbling-hair", copyright, 1923, 1951, by e.e. cummings, reprinted from, *Poems 1923-1954.* For "Death Snips Proud Men" by Carl Sandburg from *Smoke and Steel,* copyright, 1920, by Harcourt Brace Jovanovich, Inc., renewed, 1948, by Carl Sandburg.

David Higham Associates, Ltd.: For "The Party" by Reed Whittemore, an extract from *The Self Made Man* by P. Forster.

Hogarth Press Ltd.: For "Public House Confidence" by Norman Cameron from *Collected Poems.*

Holt, Rinehart and Winston, Inc.: For "Leaf Treader" by Robert Frost from *The Poetry of Robert Frost* edited by Edward Connery Lathem, copyright 1936 by Robert Frost, 1964 Lesley Frost Ballantine, 1969 by Holt, Rinehart & Winston.

Hope, Leresche & Steele: For "Goodbat Nightman" by Roger McGough, from *Penguin Modern Poets 10,* Penguin Books.

Indiana University Press: For "if" by Haroldo de Campos from *Concrete Poetry: A World View,* Mary Ellen Solt, editor,, copyright 1968 by Hispanic Arts, Indiana University.

the illustrations

Braun Electric of Canada: VIII. Harold Brillinger: 44-45, 63. John De Visser: 9, 16, 19, 20, 29, 30-31, 43-50, 51, 53, 76, 93, 100, 112, 114. Richard Harrington: 76, 100. Marburg-Art Reference Bureau: 60, 66-67. National Film Board: A Beaver, 25; G. Blouin, 22; Lutz Dille, 4, 81, 89; Ted Grant, 7, 17, 84; G. Lunney, 10, 15, 54, 64; M. Semak, 26, 56; H. Taylor, 90; Irene Taylor, 111; B. Williamson, 103; Photograph Forum: Mike Dobel, 19; Laura Jones, 13; Joan Latchford, 35, 39, 58, 78, 83, 94, 95, 105

The watercolour on page 48 is by Maria Laky.

Cover: front, National Film Board/Paul Gelinas
       back, National Film Board/ Joan Latchford

72   73   74   75   76   77   10   9   8   7   6   5   4   3